EARLY LEARN TOGETHER SERIES
DISCOVERY PLAYBOOKS
Heavy and Light

ELIZABETH LAIRD

Educational Consultant: **Carole Ritchie**

Illustrated By **Clare Beaton**

A Piccolo Original
Piccolo Books

This series has been prepared in consultation with the Pre-school Playgroups Association.

Growing heavier

Susie and Mum have taken Billy
to the clinic.
The nurse is weighing him on the scales.
She wants to find out how heavy he is.
'You're growing very nicely,' she says.
Billy likes the nurse.
He tries to grab hold of her pencil.

It's Susie's turn to be weighed now.
She's a lot heavier than Billy.
And the more she grows, the
heavier she gets.
'Doing fine,' says the nurse.

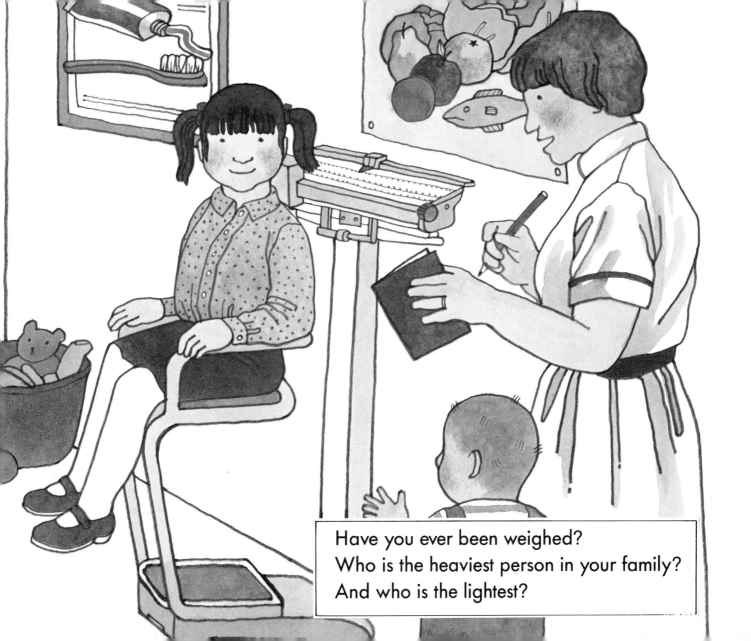

Have you ever been weighed?
Who is the heaviest person in your family?
And who is the lightest?

Weighing things

On the way home, Mum stops to buy some bananas.
'Nana!' says Billy. He likes bananas.
The greengrocer puts a nice bunch on the scales.
The black needle swings across.
He can see how much the bananas weigh.

Have you ever seen scales that look like that?

The next stop is the butcher's.
'Mince again today, is it?' asks the butcher.
Susie likes the little window on his scales.
The numbers in it go on changing, then they stop.
Mum pays the butcher and puts the meat in her bag.

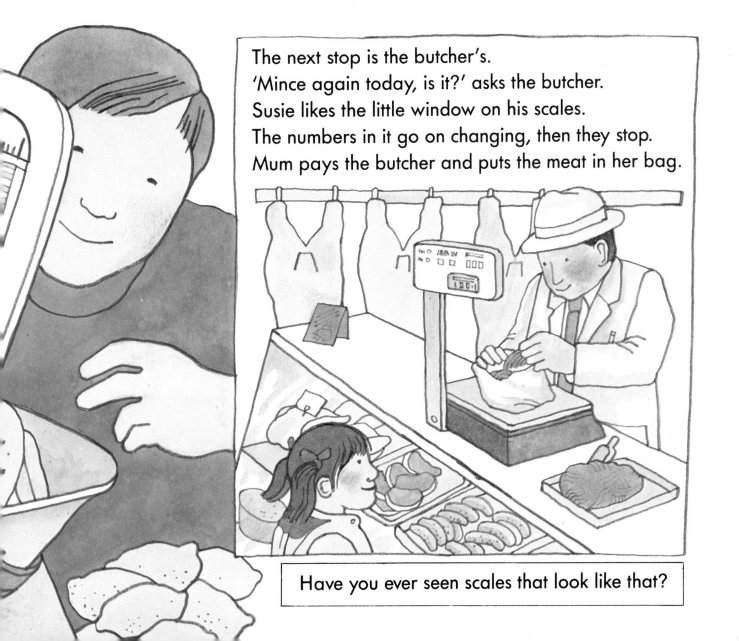

Have you ever seen scales that look like that?

Heavy things and light things

At home, everyone helps to unpack
the shopping.
Billy picks up a big tin of tomatoes.
'Careful, Billy!' says Mum. 'That's heavy.
If you drop it on your foot
it will really hurt!'

Susie's putting away the cereal.
The packet's bigger than the tin of
tomatoes, but it is much lighter.
'Look,' says Susie. 'I can carry
it in one hand.'

Look at all the shopping on the table.
Which things are heavy and
which are light?
Is the orange juice heavier than
the lettuce?
Is the rice heavier than the tea bags?

Holding up heavy weights

Oh! What a dreadful crash!
A shelf has come down in the kitchen.
Mum put some heavy tins and boxes up there,
but the shelf wasn't strong enough.
Mum will have to fix it up again.
This time she'll make sure it's stronger.

Susie's made some shelves out of an old carton,
but the top isn't strong enough to hold up her books.
Susie's cross. She hates it when things don't work.
'Never mind,' says Mum. 'Put your teddy on the top.
He's lighter than the books. He won't break it.'

Why don't you make some shelves out of a carton?

Weighing and cooking

Mum's making a cake now.
She has to weigh everything
carefully.
If she puts in too much flour,
the cake will be hard and heavy.
If she doesn't put in enough,
it will be soggy, and sink down
in the middle.

Susie is a great help.
She likes cooking.
She puts the flour and sugar
on to the scales, and
she breaks the eggs, and
stirs them in.
Billy's not very good at
cooking yet.
He's best at licking out the bowl.

Have you ever helped to weigh things on scales?

Light things move easily

It's time to go to the playground.
It's windy today, so Susie buttons up her
coat to stop the wind from
blowing it around.
Some leaves have been blown off the trees.
Even a dustbin lid has been blown
off a dustbin.
'Will the cars get blown away?' asks Susie.
'No,' says Mum. 'They're too heavy for
this wind.'

Have you ever tried blowing things away?
Put a leaf in the palm of your hand.
Can you blow it away?
Try blowing through your mouth, then
through your nose.

What about a feather? Or a stone?
Or a piece of paper? Or a spoon?

Heavy things are hard to move

There's a building site on the way
to the playground.
Susie can't take her eyes off the big crane.
'What's it for?' she says.
'It's for picking up very heavy
things,' says Mum.
'Not even the strongest man in the world could
move those big stones. But the crane can.'

Billy bounces up and down. He's seen a digger!
'Why are they using that?' asks Susie.
'It can pick up a lot of earth
at once,' says Mum.
'Much more than a man could pick
up in a shovel.'

Have you ever tried to lift up something heavy?
Have you tried to lift up a table? Or a bed?
What is the heaviest thing you can lift up?

Balancing

At the playground, Billy climbs
on to the swing.
Up he goes, and down he comes again.
Susie runs to the see-saw.
The boy on the other end is smaller
than Susie.
Susie's too heavy.
She can't make her end go up.
'Come and help me, Mum!' she shouts.

Mum presses down the boy's end to make
it as heavy as Susie's.
Down he goes and up goes Susie.

Who do you like being with on a see-saw?
A very big person? Or a very small person?
Or a person just your size?

Falling

Susie's shoe has fallen off!
It landed with quite a thump because
it's heavy.
She's dropped her ribbon too, but she
hasn't noticed.
It was so light, it landed without
a sound.

Do any of your toys make a sound when
you drop them?
Are they the light ones or the heavy ones?

While Mum was watching Susie,
Billy was turning out her bag.
Mum's knitting pattern has blown away,
and her key has fallen with a splash
into a puddle.
'I think I'd better take you
home,' says Mum,
'Before you get up to anything else!'

Try it for yourself . . .

Find a dry dishcloth, a tin of food,
a toilet roll, a bag of flour,
a bottle of water, and a plastic cup.
Put them all on the table.
Look at each one in turn,
and say 'heavy', or 'light'.
Then pick it up to test it.
Did you get them right?
Put the things in a line.
Put the heaviest at one end,
then the next heaviest,
then the next heaviest,
until you get to the lightest.

Now get some Plasticine
or some playdough.
Weigh it on the scales.
Ask Mum to help you
remember how much
it weighs.

Now make some different things.
You could make balls, and snakes, and people.
Now put everything you have make,
and all the Plasticine left over, on to the scales.
How much does it weigh?
Does it weigh the same
as it did before you broke it up?

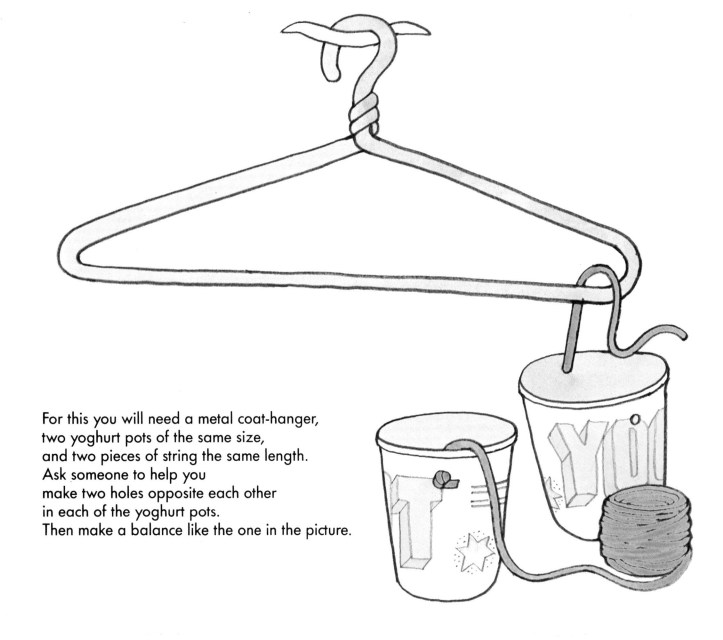

For this you will need a metal coat-hanger,
two yoghurt pots of the same size,
and two pieces of string the same length.
Ask someone to help you
make two holes opposite each other
in each of the yoghurt pots.
Then make a balance like the one in the picture.

Now put the same size teaspoon in each pot.
Hold the coat-hanger up by the hook so that the pots are hanging free.
Do they both stay level?

If they do, your balance is working properly.
If they don't, make the pieces of string longer or shorter until the balance is right.

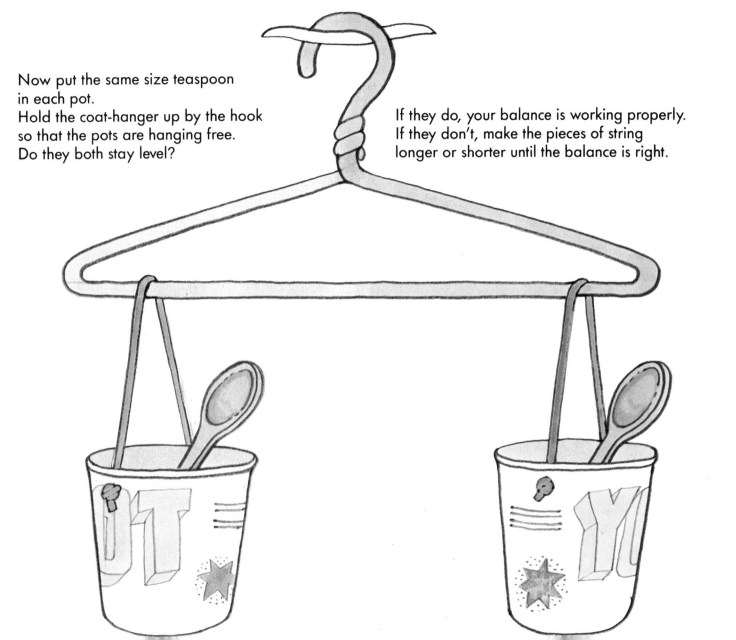

Now try putting different things into the pots,
to see which ones are heavier.
You could try a piece of Lego in one,
and a crayon in the other.
You could try weighing your toy cars,
or your farm animals, or your doll's clothes.
Try weighing lots of things,
to see which ones are heavier.

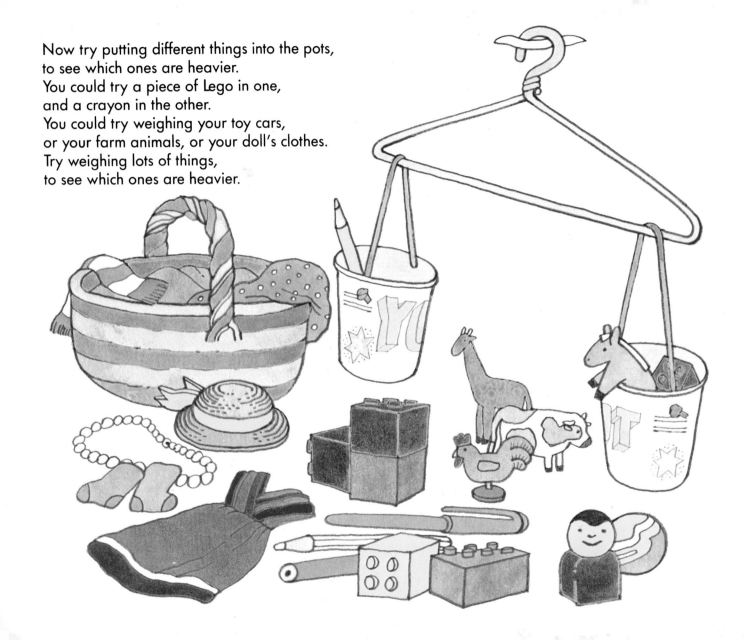